Quinn's Q Book

Qq

WRITTEN BY **J. L. MAZZEO**

ILLUSTRATED BY **HELEN ROSS REVUTSKY**

dingles &company New Jersey

©2007 by Judith Mazzeo Zocchi

First Printing

Published By dingles&company
P.O. Box 508
Sea Girt, New Jersey 08750

LIBRARY OF CONGRESS CATALOG CARD NUMBER
2005907214

ISBN
ISBN-13: 978 1-59646-512-1
ISBN-10: 1-59646-512-3

Printed in the United States of America

My Letter Library series is based on the original concept of Judy Mazzeo Zocchi.

ART DIRECTION
Barbie Lambert & Rizco Design
DESIGN
Rizco Design
EDITED BY
Andrea Curley
PROJECT MANAGER
Lisa Aldorasi
EDUCATIONAL CONSULTANT
Maura Ruane McKenna
PRE-PRESS BY
Pixel Graphics

EXPLORE THE LETTERS OF THE ALPHABET WITH MY LETTER LIBRARY*

Aimee's **A** Book
Bebe's **B** Book
Cassie's **C** Book
Delia's **D** Book
Emma's **E** Book
Faye's **F** Book
George's **G** Book
Henry's **H** Book
Izzy's **I** Book
Jade's **J** Book
Kelsey's **K** Book
Logan's **L** Book
Mia's **M** Book
Nate's **N** Book
Owen's **O** Book
Peter's **P** Book
Quinn's **Q** Book
Rosie's **R** Book
Sofie's **S** Book
Tad's **T** Book
Uri's **U** Book
Vera's **V** Book
Will's **W** Book
Xavia's **X** Book
Yola's **Y** Book
Zach's **Z** Book

* All titles also available in bilingual English/Spanish versions.

WEBSITE
www.dingles.com
E-MAIL
info@dingles.com

My **Letter** Library

Qq

My Letter Library leads young children through the alphabet one letter at a time. By focusing on an individual letter in each book, the series allows youngsters to identify and absorb the concept of each letter thoroughly before being introduced to the next. In addition, it invites them to look around and discover where objects beginning with the specific letter appear in their own world.

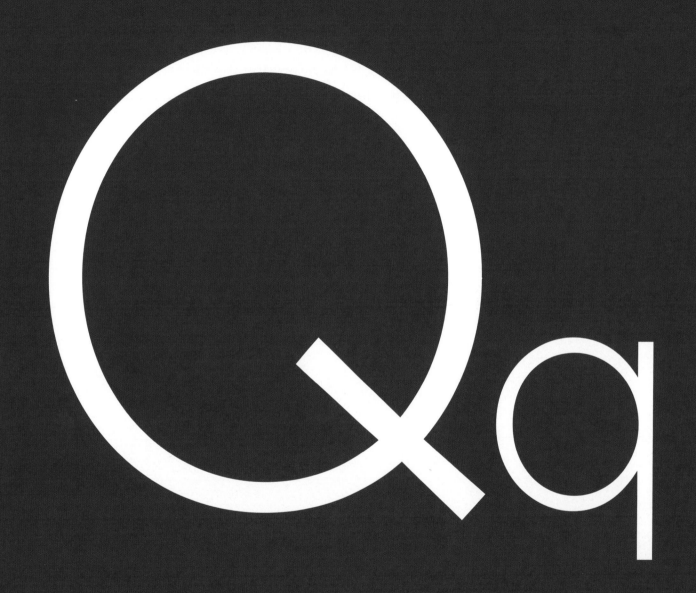

A a B b C c D d E e F f G g

H h I i J j K k L l M m N n

O o P p **Q q** R r S s T t U u

V v W w X x Y y Z z

Q is for Quinn.

Quinn is a **q**uaint **q**uail.

On Quinn's paper route
you may find
a **q**uestion mark,

Qq

a picture of the new **q**ueen,

Qq

or a **q**uarter to pay

for the paper.

Qq

While working with Quinn
you will see him wearing
a **q**uilted cape,

Qq

a hat with a **q**uill
from the beach,

Qq

and a shoulder bag

with a clasp

made of **q**uartz.

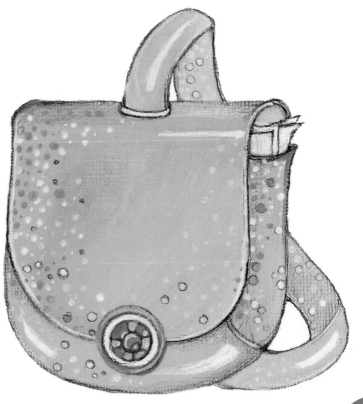

Qq

After helping Quinn
deliver the papers
you might share a
pretzel with a **q**uetzal,

Qq

enjoy a delicious **q**uince,

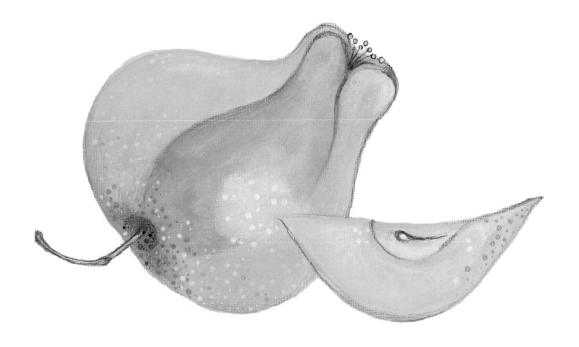

Qq

and bake a cheesy **q**uiche

for lunch.

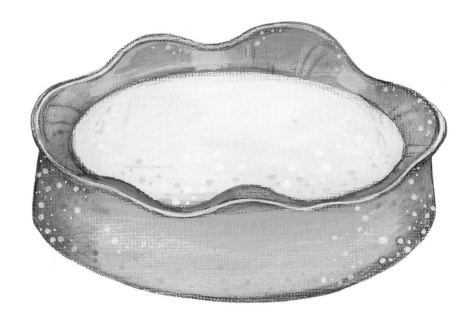

Qq

Things that begin with
the letter **Q** are all around.

QUESTION MARK

QUEEN, PICTURE

QUARTER

QUILTED CAPE

QUILL

QUARTZ **CLASP**

QUETZAL

QUINCE

QUICHE

Where on Quinn's paper route can they be found?

Have a "Q" Day!

Read "Q" stories all day long.
Read books about quails, quilts, quetzals, queens, and other **Q** words. Then have the child pick out all of the words and pictures starting with the letter **Q**.

Make a "Q" Craft: Quarter Rubbings
Collect quarters with different states depicted on the back.

Place one of the quarters beneath a piece of paper (any size will do).

Hold the quarter in place while the child rubs a crayon over the quarter.

Flip the quarter over and have the child repeat the previous step.

Encourage the child to be creative and use different-colored crayons for each Quarter Rubbing he or she does to make the rubbings into a colorful decoration!

Make a "Q" Snack: A Quilt Cake
- Make a cake according to the directions on the box. Bake it in a single rectangular cake pan.
- Let the cake cool. Then have the child ice it with white frosting, using a plastic knife.
- Now help the child divide the cake into squares by making three horizontal lines and four vertical lines on the cake with colored writing gel.
- Let the child decorate each "quilt" square differently, using raisins, M&M's, candies, fruits, and different-colored writing gels.
- Share the tasty Quilt Cake with family and friends!

For additional **"Q"** Day ideas and a reading list, go to www.dingles.com.

About **Letters**

Use the My Letter Library series to teach a child to identify letters and recognize the sounds they make by hearing them used and repeated in each story.

Ask:
- What letter is this book about?
- Can you name all of the **Q** pictures on each page?
- Which **Q** picture is your favorite? Why?
- Can you find all of the words in this book that begin with the letter **Q**?

ENVIRONMENT
Discuss objects that begin with the letter **Q** in the child's immediate surroundings and environment.

Use these questions to further the conversation:
- What coins other than a quarter make up twenty-five cents? Ask your parent to help you figure it out.
- Have you every found a quill?

- The next time your parent reads you a book, try to find as many question marks (?) as you can.

OBSERVATIONS
The My Letter Library series can be used to enhance the child's imagination. Encourage the child to look around and tell you what he or she sees.

Ask:
- Have you ever quacked like a duck?
- Can you find any **Q** objects around your home? If so, which one is your favorite?
- Have you ever tasted a quiche? Did you like it?

TRY SOMETHING NEW...
Collect as many quarters as you can and donate them to an organization that helps people in need, such as the Red Cross or the Salvation Army.

J. L. MAZZEO grew up in Middletown, New Jersey, as part of a close-knit Italian American family. She currently resides in Monmouth County, New Jersey, and still remains close to family members in heart and home.

HELEN ROSS REVUTSKY was born in St. Petersburg, Russia, where she received a degree in stage artistry/design. She worked as the directing artist in Kiev's famous Governmental Puppet Theatre. Her first book, *I Can Read the Alphabet,* was published in Moscow in 1998. Helen now lives in London, where she has illustrated several children's books.